i explore

EARTH

make
believe
ideas

WHAT'S INSIDE?

Discover more about our amazing planet!

Planet Earth

Water

Climates

olcanoes & earthquakes

Rocks & minerals

Weather: wind & storms

Weather: snow

Helping our planet

i explore facts

PLANET EARTH

Our Solar System is made up of the Earth, other planets, and the Sun. All the planets revolve around the Sun in circular paths called orbits.

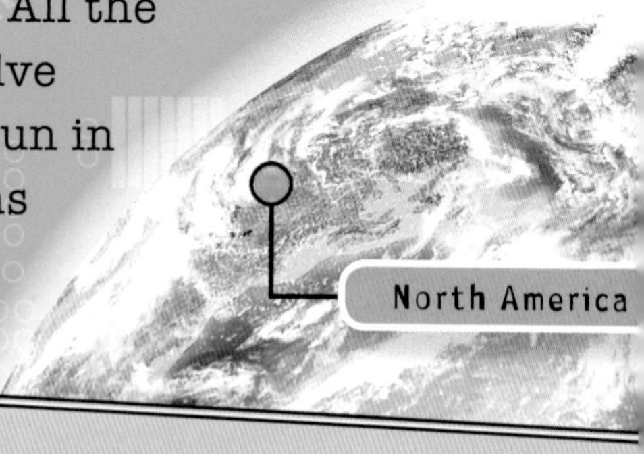

North America

Our Solar System

Earth

Venus

Jupiter

Uranus

Saturn

Neptun

Sun

Mars

Mercury

The Earth is a rocky planet made up of different layers:

- At the center of the Earth is the hot, metallic core, split into two parts: the outer core and the inner core.
- In parts of the mantle, the solid rock is so hot it melts and flows.
- The crust is the rocky outer layer.

Europe

Africa

The Earth's layers

- crust
- mantle
- outer and inner cores

i fact

ⓘ The large areas of land are called continents.

7

VOLCANOES AND EARTHQUAKES

The Earth's crust is made up of massive pieces of rock called plates. When the plates move, they can cause earthquakes and volcanic eruptions.

volcano erupting

→ i learn ✕

When the Earth's plates move apart, hot liquid rock called magma is forced up from deep underground and bursts through the crust. This makes a hole called a volcano. Magma that reaches the surface is called lava.

i discover

An earthquake happens when the Earth's plates slide past each other. A serious earthquake can cause destruction to the land and people's homes.

lava

Giant wave

i fact

Earthquakes break up
roads and create giant
waves in the ocean
called tsunamis.

A road destroyed by an earthquake

ROCKS AND MINERALS

Rocks and minerals are the materials that make up our planet. There are three main types: igneous, metamorphic, and sedimentary rock.

The Wave

i learn

This area of rock is called "The Wave." It is found in the United States and it is formed of a sedimentary rock called sandstone. Sedimentary rocks are formed from layers of hardened mud or sand. They can also contain remains of plants and animals.

i fact

ⓘ Igneous rocks, such as obsidian or basalt, form when magma cools.

Basalt columns

layers

💡 i discover

Metamorphic rocks are sedimentary or igneous rocks that have been changed into new rocks by heat or pressure. Marble is a metamorphic rock that is made from the sedimentary rock, limestone.

13

Diamonds and rubies are
examples of rare minerals
called gemstones.
They are admired for
their beauty and value.

Gemstones

WATER

Most water is held in the oceans and seas, but a small amount moves around the planet in the water cycle.

ocean

i discover

The Sun heats the sea to make water in the air called water vapor. This vapor rises to form clouds. Water then falls as rain or snow and collects together to make rivers. Rivers flow to the sea, and the water cycle begins again.

River

When flowing water drops rapidly over a rocky edge, this is called a waterfall.

Waterfall

island

There are five oceans on our planet: the Atlantic, Pacific, Indian, Southern, and Arctic. The Pacific Ocean takes up one-third of the Earth's surface and contains about 25,000 islands!

WEATHER: WIND AND STORMS

Wind, rain, sunshine, snow, and fog are different types of weather. When weather turns extreme, it can be very dangerous.

i fact

Lightning can heat the air to a temperature that is five times hotter than the surface of the Sun.

When the air moves, we feel it as wind. Hurricanes and tornadoes are very strong winds that can cause a lot of damage to the land and people's homes.

Hurricane viewed from space ⊗

cloud

forked lightning

i learn ⊗

Storm clouds can bring thunderstorms with heavy rain, thunder, and lightning. When lightning flashes from a cloud to the ground, it is called forked lightning.

i fact

In a tornado, the winds can reach 250 mph (400 kph). That's about as fast as the world's fastest sports car!

snowplow

WEATHER: SNOW

When tiny drops of water freeze, they turn into ice crystals, which then stick together to form snowflakes.

i discover

Water can also form hail. Hailstones are solid blocks of hard ice that form in cold storm clouds. They become rounded as they fall through the air.

blade

Hailstones

22

i learn

When there is a heavy snowfall, this is called a snowstorm. Roads can become blocked with snow. Snowplows use a wide blade to push snow out of the way on roads and at airports.

Snowflake

i facts

Snowflakes have six sides. No two snowflakes ever look the same.

A snowdrift is a mound of snow created by the wind. Some snowdrifts are high enough to cover a house!

CLIMATES

The climate of an area is the weather it has had for many years. The world can be divided into five different climate zones: tropical, desert, mountain, temperate, and polar.

 i discover

💡 Antarctica is the coldest place on the Earth. Both the Arctic and Antarctica have a polar climate and freezing temperatures for most of the year.

Polar landscape ⊗

 desert

(→) i learn ✗

💡 Desert climates are very hot and dry, making it tough for animals and plants to survive. The hottest place on the Earth is thought to be the Lut desert in Iran.

💡 Rain forests are found in tropical climates. They are hot and wet all year round.

Seasons are more obvious in a temperate climate. There are warm summers and cool winters.

ropical rain forest

Temperate landscape ⊗

Mountains ⊗

Tropical
Desert
Mountain
Temperate
Polar
⊗

i fact

💡 A mountain is cooler towards its top, and very little can live there. Trees can grow lower down a mountain.

HELPING OUR PLANET

The Earth provides us with a place to live, food, water, and air to breathe. By caring for our planet, we can make sure it is protected for future generations.

wind farm

➔ i learn

Coal and gas are fuels we burn to make electricity. In doing so, they give out gases that harm our planet. Using the power of the wind, waves, or sunshine, we can make electricity in a way that causes less damage to the Earth.

Landfill site

It is possible to make new things out of some of the trash we throw away. This is called recycling. By recycling, less trash will end up in giant rubbish sites called landfills.

Recycling

i facts

j By recycling one glass bottle, you can save enough energy for a lightbulb to burn for four hours.

The three chasing arrows mean that a material can be recycled.

i explore FACTS

The tallest waterfall in the world is Angel Falls in Venezuela. It is 3,212 ft (979 m) high – that's over twice the height of the Empire State Building!

Most of the planet's earthquakes occur around the edges of the Pacific Ocean. This is called the Ring of Fire, and it marks where the edges of several of the Earth's plates meet.

Clouds can be taller than our tallest mountains!

Antarctica has six months of darkness every year. During this time the Sun does not rise.

If a newspaper is recycled, it can take just one week for the recycled paper to be printed as a new newspaper.

You can only scratch a diamond using another diamond!